THE CLASSIC BOOK OF
NURSERY RHYMES

THE CLASSIC BOOK OF
NURSERY RHYMES

CRESCENT BOOKS
New York

First published in 1920 by
George G. Harrap & Co. Ltd. under the title
Mother Goose Rhymes with color plates by
S. B. Pearse and line drawings by Winifred M. Ackroyd

This edition with line drawings by Winifred M. Ackroyd
colored in by John Blackman, published in 1986 in the United States
by Crescent Books, distributed by Crown Publishers, Inc.
By arrangement with Octopus Books Limited

Printed in Hong Kong

ISBN 0 517 61669 6

OLD MOTHER GOOSE

Old Mother Goose, when
    She wanted to wander,
Would ride through the air
    On a very fine gander.

Mother Goose had a house,
    'Twas built in a wood,
Where an owl at the door
    For sentinel stood.

She had a son Jack,
    A plain-looking lad;
He was not very good,
    Nor yet very bad.

She sent him to market,
    A live goose he bought.
"Here, mother," says he,
    "It will not go for nought."

Jack's goose and her gander
    Grew very fond;
They'd both eat together,
    Or swim in one pond.

Jack found one fine morning,
    As I have been told,
His goose had laid him
    An egg of pure gold.

Jack rode to his mother,
    The news for to tell,
She called him a good boy
    And said it was well.

Jack sold his gold egg
        To a thief in disguise,
Who cheated him out of
        The half of his prize.

Then Jack went a-courting
        A lady so gay,
As fair as the lily,
        And sweet as the may.

The thief and the Squire
        Came behind his back,
And began to belabour
        The sides of poor Jack.

And then the gold egg
        Was thrown into the sea,
When Jack he jumped in,
        And got it back presently.

The thief got the goose,
        Which he vowed he would kill,
Resolving at once
        His pockets to fill.

Jack's mother came in,
     And caught the goose soon,
And mounting its back,
     Flew up to the moon.

HUMPTY-DUMPTY

Humpty-Dumpty sat on
     a wall,
Humpty-Dumpty had a
     great fall;
All the King's horses, and
     all the King's men,
Couldn't put Humpty-
     Dumpty together again.

MARY, MARY

Mary, Mary, quite contrary,
     How does your garden grow?
Silver bells and cockle-shells,
     And pretty maids all in a row.

HUSH-A-BYE, BABY

Hush-a-bye, baby, on the tree top,
When the wind blows, the cradle will rock;
When the bough bends, the cradle will fall:
Down will come baby, cradle, and all.

THREE WISE MEN OF GOTHAM

Three wise men of Gotham
Went to sea in a bowl;
If the bowl had been stronger
My story had been longer.

OLD KING COLE

Old King Cole
Was a merry old soul,
And a merry old soul was he;
And he called for his pipe,
And he called for his glass,
And he called for his fiddlers three!

THE OLD WOMAN WHO
LIVED IN A SHOE

There was an old woman who lived in
    a shoe,
She had so many children she didn't
    know what to do;
She gave them some broth, without any
    bread,
She whipped them all soundly, and sent
    them to bed.

HARK, HARK, THE DOGS DO BARK

Hark, hark,
The dogs do bark!
The beggars are coming to town,
Some in jags,
Some in rags,
And some in velvet gown.

LITTLE NANCY ETTICOTE

Little Nancy Etticote,
In a white petticoat,
With a red nose;
The longer she stands,
The shorter she grows.

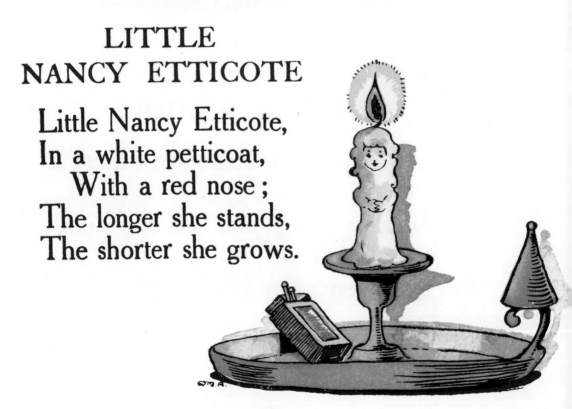

Hark, hark, the dogs do bark !

HOT CROSS BUNS

Hot cross buns, hot cross
    buns,
One a penny, two a penny,
    Hot cross buns.
If your daughters don't like
    them,
Give them to your sons,
One a penny, two a penny,
    Hot cross buns.

CHARLEY, CHARLEY

Charley, Charley, stole the barley
    Out of the baker's shop;
The baker came out, and gave him a clout,
    And made poor Charley hop.

SEE-SAW, MARGERY DAW

See-saw, Margery Daw,
Jenny shall have a new master;
She shall have but a penny a day,
Because she can't work any faster.

LITTLE POLLY FLINDERS

Little Polly Flinders
Sat among the cinders
   Warming her pretty little toes!
Her mother came and caught her,
And whipped her little daughter,
   For spoiling her nice new clothes.

DEEDLE, DEEDLE, DUMPLING

Deedle, deedle, dumpling,
   my son John,
He went to bed with his
   stockings on;
One shoe off, and one shoe
   on,
Deedle, deedle, dumpling,
   my son John.

TO MARKET, TO MARKET

To market, to market, to buy a fat pig,
    Home again, home again, jiggety jig.
To market, to market, to buy a fat hog,
    Home again, home again, jiggety jog.

THERE WAS A LITTLE MAN

There was a little man, and he had a little gun,
    And his bullets were made of lead, lead, lead;
He shot Johnny King through the middle of his wig,
    And knocked it right off his head, head, head.

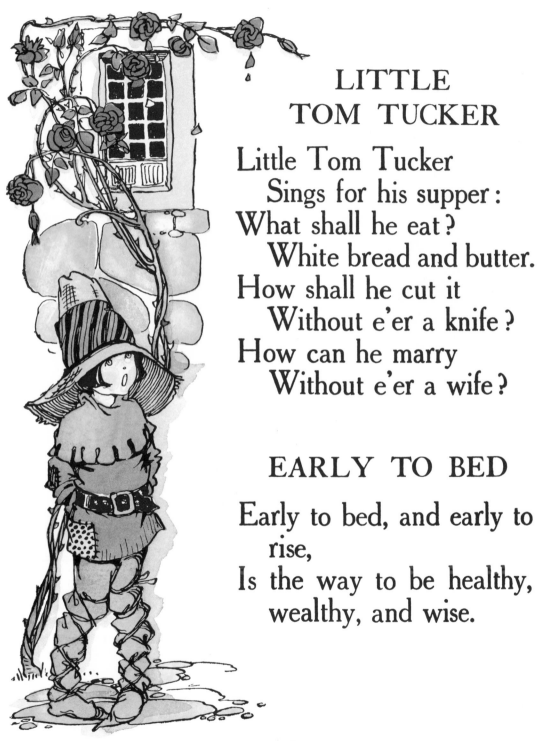

LITTLE TOM TUCKER

Little Tom Tucker
  Sings for his supper:
What shall he eat?
  White bread and butter.
How shall he cut it
  Without e'er a knife?
How can he marry
  Without e'er a wife?

EARLY TO BED

Early to bed, and early to
  rise,
Is the way to be healthy,
  wealthy, and wise.

A DILLER, A DOLLAR

A diller, a dollar, a ten o'clock
  scholar,
  What makes you come so
  soon?
You used to come at ten o'clock,
  But now you come at noon.

THE ROSE IS RED

The rose is red, the violet's
  blue;
The pink is sweet, and so
  are you.

LITTLE GIRL

Little girl, little girl, where have you
been?
Gathering roses to give to the Queen.
Little girl, little girl, what gave she you?
She gave me a diamond as big as my
shoe.

THE HOBBY-HORSE

I had a little hobby-horse,
  And it was dapple grey,
Its head was made of pea-
      straw,
  Its tail was made of hay.

I sold it to an old woman
  For a copper groat;
And I'll not sing my song
      again
Without a new coat.

22

GEORGIE PORGIE

Georgie Porgie, pudding and pie,
Kissed the girls and made them cry.
When the girls came out to play,
Georgie Porgie ran away.

YOUNG LAMBS
TO SELL

Young lambs to sell, young lambs to sell;
If I had as much money as I could tell
I never would cry, young lambs to sell,
Young lambs to sell, young lambs to sell,
I never would cry, young lambs to sell.

ROCK-A-BY

Rock-a-by, baby, thy cradle is green;
Father's a nobleman, mother's a queen;
And Betty's a lady, and wears a gold ring,
And Johnny's a drummer, and drums for
the King.

CHRISTMAS

Christmas is coming, the geese are getting fat,
Please to put a penny in an old man's hat;
If you haven't got a penny a ha'penny will do,
If you haven't got a ha'penny, God bless you.

SING, SING

Sing, sing, what shall I sing?
The cat's run away with
    the pudding-bag string!
Do, do, what shall I do?
The cat has bitten it quite
    in two.

JACK BE NIMBLE

Jack be nimble,
Jack be quick,
And Jack jump over
    the candlestick.

LITTLE MISS MUFFET

Little Miss Muffet
She sat on a tuffet,
Eating of curds and whey ;
There came a great spider,
Who sat down beside her,
And frightened Miss Muffet away.

BIRCH AND
GREEN HOLLY, BOYS

Birch and green holly, boys,
Birch and green holly.
If you get beaten, boys,
'Twill be your own folly.

THE
FIRST OF MAY

The fair maid who, the first of May,
Goes to 'the fields at break of day,
And washes in dew from the hawthorn-
    tree,
Will ever after handsome be.

THE LOST SHOE

Doodle doodle doo,
The Princess lost her
    shoe;
    Her Highness hopped,—
    The fiddler stopped,
Not knowing what to do.

AS I WAS
GOING UP
PRIMROSE
HILL

As I was going up Primrose Hill,
    Primrose Hill was dirty;
There I met a pretty Miss,
    And she dropped me a curtsey.
Little Miss, pretty Miss,
    Blessings light upon you;
If I had half-a-crown a day,
    I'd spend it all upon you.

ELSIE MARLEY

Do you ken Elsie Marley, honey,
The wife that sells the barley, honey?
She won't get up to serve her swine,
But lies in bed till eight or nine,
And surely she does take her time:
Do you ken Elsie Marley, honey?

NEEDLES AND PINS

Needles and pins, needles and pins,
When a man marries his trouble begins.

PAT-A-CAKE, BAKER'S MAN

Pat-a-cake, pat-a-cake, baker's man,
Bake me a cake as fast as you can;
Prick it and pat it, and mark it
    with G;
And put it in the oven for Teddy
    and me.

ROUND THE MULBERRY BUSH

Here we go round the mulberry bush,
The mulberry bush, the mulberry bush,
Here we go round the mulberry bush
    On a cold and frosty morning.

This is the way we wash our hands,
Wash our hands, wash our hands,
This is the way we wash our hands
    On a cold and frosty morning.

This is the way we wash our clothes,
Wash our clothes, wash our clothes,
This is the way we wash our clothes
    On a cold and frosty morning.

This is the way we go to school,
Go to school, go to school,
This is the way we go to school
    On a cold and frosty morning.

This is the way we come out of school,
Come out of school, come out of school,
This is the way we come out of school
    On a cold and frosty morning.

Here we go round the mulberry bush

I LOVE LITTLE PUSSY

I love little Pussy, her coat is so warm,
And if I don't hurt her, she'll do me no harm.
I'll sit by the fire, and give her some food,
And Pussy will love me, because I am good.

COME, LET'S TO BED

Come, let's to bed, says Sleepy-head;
Tarry a while, says Slow;
Put on the pan, says Greedy Nan,
Let's sup before we go.

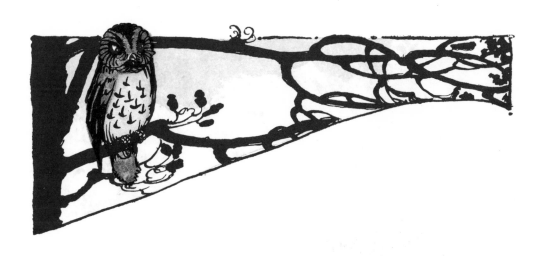

THE OWL THAT LIVED IN AN OAK

There was an Owl lived in an
    oak,
  Whiskey, Whaskey, Weedle,
And all the words he ever spoke
  Were Fiddle, Faddle, Feedle.

A sportsman chanced to come
    that way,
  Whiskey, Whaskey, Weedle;
Says he, "I'll shoot you, silly
    bird,
  So Fiddle, Faddle, Feedle!"

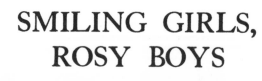

SMILING GIRLS, ROSY BOYS

Smiling girls, rosy boys,
Come and buy my little toys:
Monkeys made of gingerbread,
And sugar houses painted red.

THE ORANGE-STEALER

Dingty, diddledy, my mammy's
    maid,
She stole oranges, I'm afraid;
Some in her pockets, some in
    her sleeve,
She stole oranges, I do believe.

CRY, BABY, CRY

Cry, Baby, cry,
Put your finger in
    your eye,
And tell your mother
    it wasn't I.

SNAIL, SNAIL, COME PUT OUT YOUR HORN

Snail, snail, come put out
    your horn,
To-morrow is the day to
    shear the corn.

WHERE ARE YOU GOING TO, MY PRETTY MAID?

"Where are you going to, my pretty maid?"
"I am going a-milking, sir," she said.
"May I go with you, my pretty maid?"
"You're kindly welcome, sir," she said.
"What is your father, my pretty maid?"
"My father's a farmer, sir," she said.

"What is your fortune, my pretty maid?"
"My face is my fortune, sir," she said.
"Then I won't marry you, my pretty maid."
"Nobody asked you, sir," she said.

SATURDAY, SUNDAY

On Saturday night
  Shall be all my care
To powder my locks
  And curl my hair.

On Sunday morning
  My love will come in,
When he will marry me
  With a gold ring.

LITTLE TOMMY TITTLE-MOUSE

Little Tommy Tittlemouse
Lived in a little house;
He caught fishes
In other men's ditches.

MOLLY, MY SISTER, AND I
FELL OUT

Molly, my sister, and I fell out,
And what do you think it was about?
She loved coffee, and I loved tea,
And that was the reason we couldn't agree.

THE LITTLE NUT TREE

I had a little nut tree; nothing would it bear
But a silver nutmeg and a golden pear.
The King of Spain's daughter came to see me,
And all was because of my little nut tree.
I skipped over water, I danced over sea,
And all the birds in the air couldn't catch me.

I HAD A LITTLE WIFE

I had a little wife, the prettiest
  ever seen,
She washed up the dishes
  and kept the house clean;

She went to the mill to fetch
  me some flour,
She brought it home safe in
  less than an hour;

She baked me my bread, she
  brewed me my ale;
She sat by the fire and told
  me a tale.

BYE, BABY BUNTING

Bye, Baby Bunting,
Father's gone a-hunting,
Mother's gone a-milking,
Sister's gone a-silking,
Brother's gone to buy a skin
To wrap the Baby Bunting in.

DANCE TO YOUR DADDY

Dance to your daddy,
My little babby;
Dance to your daddy,
My little lamb.
You shall have a fishy,
In a little dishy;
You shall have a fishy,
When the boat comes
    in.

LAVENDER AND ROSEMARY

Lavender blue and rosemary green,
When I am king you shall be queen;
Call up my maids at four o'clock,
Some to the wheel and some to the rock,
Some to make hay and some to shear corn,
And you and I will keep ourselves warm.

SNEEZING

If you sneeze on Monday, you sneeze for danger;
Sneeze on Tuesday, kiss a stranger;
Sneeze on Wednesday, sneeze for a letter;
Sneeze on Thursday, something better;
Sneeze on Friday, sneeze for sorrow;
Sneeze on Saturday, see your sweetheart to-
morrow.

OF WASHING

They that wash on Friday,
Wash in need;
And they that wash on Saturday,
Oh! they are sluts indeed.

RAIN, RAIN, GO TO SPAIN

Rain, rain, go to Spain,
And never come back again.

POLLY AND SUKEY

Polly, put the kettle on,
Polly, put the kettle on,
Polly, put the kettle on,
    And we'll have tea.
Sukey, take it off again,
Sukey, take it off again,
Sukey, take it off again,
    They're all gone away.

LITTLE MAID

"Little maid, pretty maid,
    whither goest thou?"
"Down in the forest to
    milk my cow."
"Shall I go with thee?"
    "No, not now;
When I send for thee, then
    come thou."

THE PUMPKIN-EATER

Peter, Peter, pumpkin-eater,
Had a wife and couldn't
    keep her;
He put her in a pumpkin
    shell,
And there he kept her very
    well.

BOUNCE, BUCKRAM

Bounce, buckram,
    velvet's dear,
Christmas comes but
    once a year.

GOOSEY, GOOSEY, GANDER

Goosey, goosey, gander, whither shall I wander,
Upstairs, and downstairs, and in my lady's
    chamber.
There I met an old man, who would not say his
    prayers,
I took him by his left leg, and threw him down
    the stairs.

SOLOMON GRUNDY

Solomon Grundy,
Born on a Monday,
Christened on Tuesday,
Married on Wednesday,
Very ill on Thursday,

Worse on Friday,
Died on Saturday,
Buried on Sunday.
This is the end
Of Solomon Grundy.

RIDE A COCK-HORSE

Ride a cock-horse
To Banbury Cross,
To see a fine lady
Upon a white horse.

Rings on her fingers,
Bells on her toes,
She shall have music
Wherever she goes.

THE QUEEN OF HEARTS

The Queen of Hearts
She made some tarts
All on a summer's day;
The Knave of Hearts
He stole those tarts,
And took them clean away.

The King of Hearts
Called for the tarts,
And beat the Knave full
sore;
The Knave of Hearts
Brought back the tarts,
And vowed he'd steal no
more.

THE MAN IN THE MOON

The man in the moon
Came tumbling down,
And asked the way to Norwich;
He went by the south,
And burnt his mouth
With eating cold pease porridge.

I HAD A LITTLE PONY

I had a little pony;
　　They called him Dapple-grey.
I lent him to a lady,
　　To ride a mile away.
She whipped him, she slashed him,
　　She rode him through the mire;
I would not lend my pony now,
　　For all the lady's hire.

TWO PIGEONS

I had two pigeons bright
  and gay,
They flew from me the
  other day.
What was the reason they
  did go?
I cannot tell, for I do not
  know.

SNAIL, SNAIL

Snail, snail, come out of
  your hole,
Or else I'll beat you as
  black as a coal.

HEY, DIDDLE, DIDDLE

Hey, diddle, diddle, the cat and the
fiddle,
The cow jumped over the moon ;
The little dog laughed to see such sport,
And the dish ran away with the
spoon.

THE CROOKED MAN

There was a crooked man, and he went a
    crooked mile,
And he found a crooked sixpence against
    a crooked stile;
He bought a crooked cat, which caught a
    crooked mouse;
And they all lived together in a little
    crooked house.

SLEEP, BABY,
SLEEP

Sleep, baby, sleep,
Our cottage vale is deep:
The little lamb is on the green,
With woolly fleece so soft and clean—
　　Sleep, baby, sleep.

Sleep, baby, sleep,
Down where the woodbines creep;
Be always like the lamb so mild,
A kind, and sweet, and
　　　　gentle child.
　　Sleep, baby, sleep.

PEASE PUDDING
HOT

Pease pudding hot,
　　Pease pudding cold,
Pease pudding in the pot,
　　Nine days old.

Some like it hot,
　　Some like it cold,
Some like it in the pot,
　　Nine days old.

61

LITTLE BOY BLUE

Little Boy Blue, come, blow me your horn;
The sheep's in the meadow, the cow's in the corn.
Where's the little boy that looks after the sheep?
He's under the haycock, fast asleep.

THREE MEN IN A TUB

Rub-a-dub-dub!
Three men in a tub;
And what do you think
    they be?
The butcher, the
    baker,
The candlestick-
    maker;
Turn 'em out knaves
    all three!

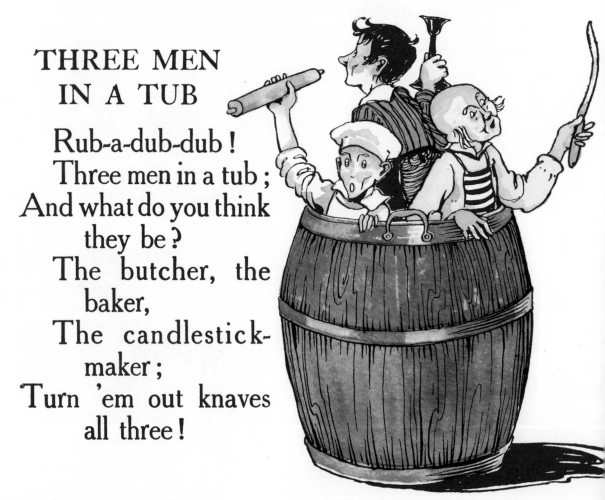

AS TOMMY SNOOKS AND BESSY BROOKS

As Tommy Snooks and Bessy Brooks
Were walking out one Sunday,
Says Tommy Snooks to Bessy Brooks
Wilt marry me on Monday?

DING,
DONG,
BELL

Ding, dong, bell,
Pussy's in the well.
Who put her in?
Little Tommy Green.
Who pulled her out?
Little Tommy Trout.
What a naughty boy was that,
Thus to drown poor Pussy Cat!

DICKERY, DICKERY, DOCK

Dickery, dickery, dock!
The mouse ran up the clock;
The clock struck one, and down
     the mouse ran,
Dickery, dickery, dock.

IF WISHES WERE HORSES

If wishes were horses, beggars would ride,
If turnips were watches, I would wear one
     by my side.

JACK AND JILL

Jack and Jill went up the hill
    To fetch a pail of water ;
Jack fell down and broke his crown,
    And Jill came tumbling after.

Up Jack got, and home did trot,
    As fast as he could caper ;

Dame Jill had the job to plaister his knob,
　With vinegar and brown paper.

Jill came in and she did grin
　To see his paper plaister,
Mother vexed did whip her next,
　For causing Jack's disaster.

DANCE, LITTLE BABY

Dance, little Baby, dance up high!
Never mind, Baby, Mother is by;
Crow and caper, caper and crow,
There, little Baby, there you go!
Up to the ceiling, down to the
　　ground,
Backwards and forwards, round
　　and round;
Dance, little Baby, and Mother
　　will sing,
With the merry coral, ding, ding,
　　ding!

TAFFY WAS A WELSHMAN

Taffy was a Welshman,
　Taffy was a thief,
Taffy came to my house
　And stole a leg of
　　beef.

I went to Taffy's house,
　Taffy was not at home;
Taffy came to my house
　And stole a marrow-
　　bone.

I went to Taffy's house,
  Taffy was in bed;
I took the marrow-bone
  And broke Taffy's head.

GREEN GRAVEL

Around the green gravel the grass grows green,
And all the pretty maids are plain to be seen;
Wash them with milk, and clothe them with silk,
And write their names with a pen and ink.

LITTLE JUMPING JOAN

Here am I, Little Jumping Joan,
When nobody's with me, I'm always alone.

THE TAILORS AND THE SNAIL

Four and twenty tailors went to kill a snail,
The best man amongst them durst not touch her tail.
She put out her horns, like a little Kyloe cow,
Run, tailors, run, or she'll kill you all just now.

QUEEN ANNE

Queen Anne, Queen Anne, she sits in the sun,
As fair as the lily, as white as the swan:
I send you three letters, so pray you read one.
I cannot read one unless I read all;
So pray, Master Teddy, deliver the ball.

THE SQUIRREL

The winds they did blow,
　　The leaves they did wag;
Along came a beggar-boy,
　　And put me in his bag.

He took me up to London:
　　A lady did me buy;
Put me in a silver cage,
　　And hung me up on high.

With apples by the fire,
　　And nuts for to crack:
　　　Besides a little feather-
　　　　bed
　　　　　To rest my little
　　　　　back.

OLD FARMER GILES

Old Farmer Giles
He went seven miles,
With his faithful dog, Old Rover;
And Old Farmer Giles,
When he came to the stiles,
Took a run and jumped clean over.

BA-A, BA-A, BLACK SHEEP

Ba-a, ba-a, black sheep, have you any wool?
Yes, sir, yes, sir, three bags full:
One for my master, one for my dame,
And one for the little boy that lives in our lane.
Ba-a, ba-a, black sheep, have you any wool?
Yes, sir, yes, sir, three bags full.

LITTLE JACK HORNER

Little Jack Horner
Sat in a corner,
Eating a Christmas pie;
He put in his thumb,
And he took out a plum,
And said, "What a good
boy am I!"

ONE, TWO, BUCKLE MY SHOE

One, two, buckle my shoe;
Three, four, shut the door;
Five, six, pick up sticks;

Seven, eight, lay them straight;
Nine, ten, a good fat hen;
Eleven, twelve, dig and delve;
Thirteen, fourteen, maids a-courting;
Fifteen, sixteen, maids in the kitchen;
Seventeen, eighteen, maids in waiting;
Nineteen, twenty, my plate is empty.

FIVE TOES

This little pig went to market;
This little pig stayed at home;
This little pig had roast meat;
This little pig had none;
This pig went to the barn door
And cried "Week, week," for
more.

THERE WAS AN OLD WOMAN

There was an old woman lived under a hill,
And if she's not gone, she lives there still.

OLD MOTHER WIDDLE WADDLE

Old Mother Widdle Waddle jumped out of bed,
And out of the casement she popped her head,
Crying, "The house is on fire, the grey goose is dead,
And the fox has come to the town, oh!"

BOYS AND GIRLS,
COME OUT
TO PLAY

Boys and girls, come out to play,
The moon does shine as bright as day;
   Leave your supper, and leave your sleep,
   And meet your playfellows in the street;

Come with a whoop, and come with a call,
And come with a good will, or not at all.
Up the ladder and down the wall,
A halfpenny loaf will serve us all.
You find milk and I'll find flour,
And we'll have a pudding in half an hour.

LITTLE
BETTY BLUE

Little Betty Blue
Lost her holiday shoe:
What can little Betty do?
Give her another
To match the other,
And then she may walk
in two.

THE NORTH WIND
DOTH BLOW

The North Wind doth blow,
And we shall have snow,
And what will poor Robin do then,
    Poor thing?

He will hop to a barn,
And to keep himself warm,
Will hide his head under his wing,
    Poor thing!

WHEN I WAS
A BACHELOR

When I was a bachelor, I lived by myself,
And all the meat I got I put upon a shelf;
The rats and the mice did lead me such a life,
That I went to London, to get myself a wife.

The streets were so broad, and the lanes were so
     narrow,
I could not get my wife home without a wheelbarrow.
The wheelbarrow broke, my wife got a fall,
Down tumbled wheelbarrow, little wife, and all.

THE BUNCH OF BLUE RIBBONS

Oh dear, what can the matter be?
Oh dear, what can the matter be?
Oh dear, what can the matter be?
Johnny's so long at the fair.

He promised he'd buy me a bunch
of blue ribbons,
He promised he'd buy me a bunch
of blue ribbons,
He promised he'd buy me a bunch
of blue ribbons,
To tie up my bonnie brown hair.

POOR OLD
ROBINSON CRUSOE!

Poor old Robinson
Crusoe!
Poor old Robinson
Crusoe!
They made him a coat of
an old Nanny goat,
I wonder how they could
do so!
With a ring-a-ting-tang, and
a ring-a-ting-tang,
Poor old Robinson
Crusoe!

LITTLE BO-PEEP

Little Bo-peep has lost her sheep,
    And cannot tell where to find them ;
Leave them alone, and they'll come home,
    And bring their tails behind them.

Little Bo-peep fell fast asleep,
    And dreamt she heard them bleating ;
But when she awoke she found it a joke,
    For still they all were fleeting.

Then up she took her little crook,
    Determined for to find them ;
She found 'em indeed, but it made her heart bleed,
    For they'd left their tails behind 'em.

It happened one day, as Bo-peep did stray
    Unto a meadow hard by,
There she espied their tails, side by side,
    All hung on a tree to dry.

Then she heaved a sigh, and wiped her eye,
    And ran o'er hill and dale-o,
And tried what she could, as a shepherdess should,
    To tack to each sheep its tail-o.

UP STREET,
AND
DOWN STREET

Up street, and down street,
    Each window's made of glass;
If you go to Tommy Tickler's house
    You'll find a pretty lass.

I SAW A SHIP
A-SAILING

I saw a ship a-sailing,
    A-sailing on the sea ;
And, oh ! it was all laden
    With pretty things for thee !

There were comfits in the cabin,
    And apples in the hold ;
The sails were made of silk,
    And the masts were made of gold.

The four and twenty sailors
    That stood between the decks,
Were four and twenty white mice,
    With chains about their necks.

The captain was a duck,
    With a packet on his back;
And when the ship began to move,
    The captain said, "Quack! quack!"

PUSSY CAT, PUSSY CAT

Pussy cat, Pussy cat,
    where have you
    been?
I've been to London to
    look at the Queen.
Pussy cat, Pussy cat,
    what did you do
    there?
I frightened a little
    mouse under the
    chair.

ROBIN AND RICHARD

Robin and Richard were two pretty men,
They lay in bed till the clock struck ten;
Then up starts Robin and looks in the
    sky,
"Oh, brother Richard, the sun's very
    high!
You go on with bottle and bag,
And I'll come after with jolly Jack
    Nag."

Monday's Child is Fair of Face

A WEEK OF BIRTHDAYS

Monday's child is fair of face,
Tuesday's child is full of grace,
Wednesday's child is full of woe,
Thursday's child has far to go,
Friday's child is loving and giving,
Saturday's child works hard for its living,
But the child that is born on the Sabbath
    day
Is bonny and blithe, and good and gay.

TO MARKET, TO MARKET

To market, to market, to
buy a plum cake;
Home again, home again,
market is late.
To market, to market, to
buy a plum bun;
Home again, home again,
market is done.

ST IVES

As I was going to St Ives,
I met a man with seven wives,
Every wife had seven sacks,
Every sack had seven cats,
Every cat had seven kits:

Kits, cats, sacks, and wives,
How many were there going
to St Ives?

LITTLE BOY, PRETTY BOY

Little boy, pretty boy, where were you born?
In Lincolnshire, master; come, blow the cow's
horn.

MY
MAID MARY

My maid Mary she minds
the dairy,
While I go a-hoeing and
mowing each morn.
Gaily run the reel and the
little spinning-wheel,
Whilst I am singing and
mowing my corn.

HINK, MINX!

Hink, minx! the old witch winks,
The fat begins to fry.
There's nobody at home but
jumping Joan,
Father, mother, and I.

CROSS-PATCH, DRAW
THE LATCH

Cross-patch,
Draw the latch,
Sit by the fire and spin,
Take a cup,
And drink it up,
And call your neighbours in.

93

THERE WAS AN OLD WOMAN

There was an old woman
    tossed up in a basket,
Ninety times as high as
    the moon ;
And where she was going,
    I couldn't but ask it,
For in her hand she carried
    a broom.

"Old woman, old woman, old woman,"
    quoth I,
    "O whither, O whither, O whither
    so high ? "
"To sweep the cobwebs off the sky !"
    "Shall I go with you ? "   "Ay, by-
    and-by."

SING A SONG OF SIXPENCE

Sing a song of sixpence,
  A pocket full of rye;
Four and twenty black-
  birds
  Baked in a pie;
When the pie was opened,
  The birds began to sing,
Was not that a dainty dish
  To set before the King?

The King was in his
  counting-house,
  Counting out his money;
The Queen was in the parlour,
  Eating bread and honey;
The maid was in the garden,
  Hanging out the clothes;
Up came a little bird,
  And snapt off her nose.

CURLY-LOCKS, CURLY-LOCKS

Curly-locks, Curly-locks, wilt thou be mine?
Thou shalt not wash the dishes, nor yet feed
    the swine;
But sit on a cushion, and sew a fine seam,
And feed upon strawberries, sugar, and cream.

WEE WILLIE WINKIE

Wee Willie Winkie
    runs through the
    town,
Upstairs and down-
    stairs in his night-
    gown;
Rapping at the window,
    crying through the
    lock,
"Are the children in
    their beds, for it's
    past eight o'clock?"

THREE BLIND MICE

Three blind mice! see how they run!
They all run after the farmer's wife,
Who cut off their tails with a carving
    knife,
Did ever you see such a thing in your
    life as three blind mice?

TWINKLE, TWINKLE, LITTLE STAR

Twinkle, twinkle, little star,
How I wonder what you are!
Up above the world so high,
Like a diamond in the sky.

When the blazing sun is gone,
When he nothing shines upon,
Then you show your little light,
Twinkle, twinkle, all the night.

Then the traveller in the dark
Thanks you for your tiny spark:
How could he see where to go,
If you did not twinkle so?

In the dark blue sky you keep,
Often through my curtains peep,
For you never shut your eye,
Till the sun is in the sky.

As your bright and tiny spark
Lights the traveller in the dark,
Though I know not what you are,
Twinkle, twinkle, little star.

THREE STRAWS ON A STAFF

Three straws on a staff,
Would make a baby cry and laugh.

THE
FAT MAN
OF
BOMBAY

There was a fat man of Bombay,
Who was smoking one sunshiny day,
When a bird called a Snipe flew away with
his pipe,
Which vexed the fat man of Bombay.

RAIN,
RAIN,
GO
AWAY

Rain, rain, go away,
Come again April day;
Little Johnny wants to play.

APPLE-PIE

Apple-pie, pudding, and pancake,
All begins with A.

TOM, TOM, THE PIPER'S SON

Tom, Tom, the piper's son,
Stole a pig, and away he run.
The pig was eat, and Tom was beat,
And Tom ran crying down the street.

I SAW THREE SHIPS

I saw three ships come sailing by,
 Sailing by, sailing by,
I saw three ships come sailing by
 On New Year's Day in the morning.

Three pretty girls were in them then,
 In them then, in them then,
Three pretty girls were in them then,
 On New Year's Day in the morning.

Winifred M. Ackroyd.

GREAT A, LITTLE A

Great A, little A,
   Bouncing B,
The cat's in the cupboard,
   And can't see me.

THE COCK DOTH CROW

The Cock doth crow to let you know,
If you be wise, 'tis time to rise.

PLEASE TO REMEMBER

Please to remember the fifth of
      November,
  The Gunpowder treason plot;
I see no reason why Gunpowder
      treason
  Should ever be forgot.
A stick and a stake for Victoria's sake,
Hollo, boys! hollo, boys! God save
     the Queen!

I LOVE SIXPENCE

I love sixpence, pretty little
    sixpence,
  I love sixpence better
    than my life;
I spent a penny of it, I spent
    another,
  And took fourpence
    home to my wife.

    Oh, my little fourpence, pretty little
       fourpence,
      I love fourpence better than my
        life;
    I spent a penny of it, I spent another,
      And I took twopence home to my
       wife.

Oh, my little twopence, my pretty little twopence,
  I love twopence better than my life;
I spent a penny of it, I spent another,
  And I took nothing home to my wife.

Oh, my little nothing, my pretty little nothing,
  What will nothing buy for my wife?
I have nothing, I spend nothing,
  I love nothing better than my wife.

DOCTOR FOSTER

Doctor Foster went to
    Glo'ster,
In a shower of rain;
He stepped in a puddle,
    up to the middle,
And never went there
    again.

THE LITTLE GIRL WHO HAD A CURL

There was a little girl who had a little curl
Right in the middle of her forehead;
When she was good, she was very, very good,
And when she was bad she was horrid.

DAFFY-DOWN-DILLY

Daffy-down-dilly has come up to town,
In a yellow petticoat and a green gown.

LUCY LOCKET

Lucy Locket
Lost her pocket,
Kitty Fisher
    Found it;

Nothing in it,
Nothing in it,
But the binding
    Round it.

DAME, GET UP

Dame, get up and bake
  your pies,
Bake your pies, bake your
  pies;
Dame, get up and bake
  your pies,
On Christmas Day in the
  morning.

Dame, what makes your
  maidens lie,
Maidens lie, maidens
  lie;
Dame, what makes your maidens lie,
On Christmas Day in the morning?

Dame, what makes your ducks to die,
Ducks to die, ducks to die;
Dame, what makes your ducks to die,
On Christmas Day in the morning?

110

Their wings are cut and they cannot
    fly,
Cannot fly, cannot fly;
Their wings are cut and they cannot
    fly,
On Christmas Day in the morning.

PETER PIPER

Peter Piper picked
  a peck of pickled
  pepper;
A peck of pickled
  pepper Peter
  Piper picked.
If Peter Piper picked
  a peck of pickled
  pepper,
Where's the peck
  of pickled pep-
  per Peter Piper
  picked?

JACK SPRAT

Jack Sprat could eat no fat,
　　His wife could eat no lean ;
And so betwixt them both, you see,
　　They licked the platter clean.

THE RUSTY MILLER

Oh, the rusty, dusty, rusty miller,
I'll not change my wife for gold or silver.

EVENING RED AND
MORNING GREY

Evening red and morning grey,
It is the sign of a bonnie day;
Evening grey and morning red,
The lamb and the ewe go wet
to bed.

SIMPLE SIMON

Simple Simon met a
pieman,
Going to the fair;
Says Simple Simon to
the pieman,
"Let me taste your
ware."

Says the pieman to
Simple Simon,
"Show me first
your penny."
Says Simple Simon to the pieman,
"Indeed I have not any."

He went to catch a dickey-bird,
And thought he could not fail,
Because he'd got a little salt
To put upon its tail.

He went to take a bird's nest,
    Was built upon a bough:
A branch gave way, and Simon fell
    Into a dirty slough.

He went to shoot a wild duck,
    But wild duck flew away;
Says Simon, "I can't hit him,
    Because he will not stay."

Simple Simon went a-hunting,
    For to catch a hare;
He rode an ass about the streets,
    But couldn't find one there.

Simple Simon went a-fishing
    For to catch a whale;
All the water he had got
    Was in his mother's pail.

He went for to eat honey
    Out of the mustard-pot;
He bit his tongue until he cried,
    That was all the good he got.

He went to ride a spotted cow,
    That had a little calf,
She threw him down upon the ground,
    Which made the people laugh.

Once Simon made a great snowball,
    And brought it in to roast;
He laid it down before the fire,
    And soon the ball was lost.

He went to slide upon the ice,
    Before the ice would bear;
Then he plunged in above his knees,
    Which made poor Simon stare.

He washed himself with blacking-ball,
    Because he had no soap;
Then said unto his mother,
    "I'm a beauty now, I hope."

Simple Simon went to look
    If plums grew on a thistle;
He pricked his fingers very much,
    Which made poor Simon whistle.

He went for water in a sieve,
    But soon it all ran through;
And now poor Simple Simon
    Bids you all adieu.

HERE COMES A POOR WOMAN

Here comes a poor woman from Babyland,
With three small children in her hand:
One can brew, another can bake,
The other can make a pretty round cake.
One can sit in the garden and spin,
Another can make a fine bed for the king;
Pray, ma'am, will you take one in?

LITTLE
POLL
PARROT

Little Poll Parrot
Sat in her garret,
Eating toast and tea;
A little brown mouse
Jumped into the house,
And stole it all away.

MARY'S LAMB

Mary had a little lamb,
    Its fleece was white as snow;
And everywhere that Mary went
    The lamb was sure to go.

THERE WAS A RAT

There was a Rat, for want of stairs,
Went down a rope to say his prayers.

119

THE DEATH AND BURIAL OF
POOR COCK ROBIN

Who killed Cock Robin?
  I, said the Sparrow,
  With my bow and arrow,
I killed Cock Robin.

Who saw him die?
  I, said the Fly,
  With my little eye,
I saw him die.

Who caught his blood?
  I, said the Fish,
  With my little dish,
I caught his blood.

Who'll make his shroud?
  I, said the Beetle,
  With my thread and needle,
I'll make his shroud.

Who'll dig his grave?
  I, said the Owl,
  With my spade and shovel,
I'll dig his grave.

Who'll be the Parson?
  I, said the Rook,
  With my little book,
I'll be the Parson.

Who'll be the Clerk?
  I, said the Lark,
  If it's not in the dark,
I'll be the Clerk.

Who'll carry him to the grave?
  I, said the Kite,
  If it's not in the night,
I'll carry him to the grave.

Who'll carry the link?
  I, said the Linnet,
  I'll fetch it in a minute,
I'll carry the link.

Who'll be chief mourner?
  I, said the Dove,
  For I mourn for my love,
I'll be chief mourner.

Who'll sing a psalm?
  I, said the Thrush,
  As she sat in a bush,
I'll sing a psalm.

Who'll toll the bell?
    I, said the Bull,
    Because I can pull;
So, Cock Robin, farewell!

All the birds of the air
    Fell a-sighing and sobbing
When they heard the bell toll
    For poor Cock Robin.

LADYBIRD, LADYBIRD

Ladybird, Ladybird, fly away home,
Your house is on fire, your children will burn.

Index of the Rhymes